Albert Clayton's
FORGOTTEN FYLDE
Album

MARKET PLACE GARSTANG.

Wyre Publishing
North Villas, Garstang Road, St Michael's on Wyre, Lancashire, PR3 0TE.

Above: *GARSTANG, Bridge Street, 1903:* Photograph by Herbert Jackson of Cleckheaton. Richard Lang's Motor and Cycle repair works is seen on the right of the photograph; it was situated next door to Ivy Cottage where he lived with his family.

Above: *GARSTANG, The Market Place, c.1892:* Photograph by Herbert Jackson of Cleckheaton, who was formerly a Garstang photographer. The office on the left of the picture was owned by William Blackhurst, a respected 19th century solicitor, practising in Preston, Garstang and Blackpool. (It is still a solicitor's office in the ownership of Blackhurst, Parker & Yates.) The business was taken over in 1852 by his son William, who had eleven children - one of whom, Alfred, his sixth son, was admitted a solicitor in 1894, and went into partnership with his father who died in February 1904. Alfred's sons, William and Bernard, later joined the family business as solicitors, and became Coroner and Deputy Coroner respectively. Hartley's ironmonger's shop, seen in the centre background, was previously owned by Richard Cliffe, who was a tinsmith and ironmonger in Garstang Market Place from c.1828. The business was taken over c.1865 by Joseph Hartley who sold it to Henry Singleton in 1902.

ALBERT CLAYTON'S

CONTENTS

AUTHOR'S ACKNOWLEDGEMENTS

The publication of this book would not have been possible without the assistance of many people, some of whom have provided me with valuable information for the captions, whilst others have loaned me a number of their treasured photographs. My special thanks are due to my wife Margaret, and to William (Bill) Elless Hodgson for reading the text and for his helpful suggestions. My grateful thanks are due to Michael J. Fitzherbert-Brockholes, Esq., John and Annie Bainbridge, Alan Bamber, Jim and Elsie Clark, David and Julie Cliff, Alvin Cook, Lottie and the late 'Ted' Cutler, Jim and Elizabeth Eccleston, John Gornall, Denis Holborn, Annie Jackson, Bill and Annie Mason, Margaret Moss, Jim and Edna Parker, Elizabeth Pickup, Annie Rowe, Annie Steele, Mary Swarbrick, Betty Thackeray, John Wainman.

BIBLIOGRAPHY

A tour through the Northern Counties of England and the Borders of Scotland, Rev. R. Warner
Deeds of Goosnargh Mill
Garstang Deanery Magazines (1892 - 1896)
Maritime Heritage, Barrow & Morecambe Bay, Raymond Sankey
Moore's Almanac, 1815
Northward, Anthony Hewitson
Our Country Churches & Chapels, Atticus
Pilling Parish Magazines (1870 - 1873)
Preston & Wyre Railway - original documents
St. Michael's on Wyre Museum Catalogue
St. Michael's on Wyre Parish Registers
The Blackpool Times & Fylde Observer
The Fleetwood Chronicle, Fylde News & Advertiser
The Lancaster Gazette
The Preston Chronicle
The Preston Guardian
The Preston Herald
The Preston Pilot
The Village Labourer, J .L. & B. Hammond

FRONT COVER: POULTON le FYLDE, Ebeneezer Richards's Hardware store, Market Place, c.1904:

FRONT COVER: BONDS, Garstang Corn Mill, c.1910: Photograph by Crosland of Lancaster.

INNER FRONT COVER: GARSTANG, 6 April 1899: Invoice from Nicholas Isles, landlord of the Royal Oak Hotel, to a Mr. Jenkinson for a Landau and pair to Scorton Church. Note that Nicholas Isles also hired out hearses.

TITLE PAGE: GARSTANG, Market Day, 1908: In 1897, the Market Place was illuminated by fitting two gas lamps to the Obelisk which commemorated the Diamond Jubilee of Her Majesty Queen Victoria. The cost of the work caused great concern amongst the residents of Garstang. The general opinion was that £5 would be a suitable cost when compared with fitting other gas lamps round the town. The cleaning of the Obelisk, fixing an inscribed plaque, and the fitting of the lamps with brackets, cost £40 - a sum which staggered the townsfolk. It was thought that since it was Queen Victoria's Diamond Jubilee, some of the money had been 'sunk in the well'.

Copyright © Albert Clayton/Wyre Publishing

Typesetting by Highlight Type Bureau Ltd, Bradford and printed in the United Kingdom by The Amadeus Press Ltd, Huddersfield.

INTRODUCTION

Above: *GARSTANG, Coronation Day, 22nd June 1911:* **Photograph by A. E. Shaw of Blackburn: A busy scene in front of the Royal Oak Hotel during the celebrations marking the Coronation of King George V and Queen Mary. In the evening, a race was run from the Royal Oak Hotel to the Bourne Arms Hotel at Knott End - a distance of some 11 miles. The race was won by Mr. Brocklebank of Preesall in the respectable time of 1 hour and 8 minutes - one and a half minutes ahead of John Parkinson of Preesall with Thomas Swarbrick of Garstang in third place.**

At the time the following photographs were produced, many of which date back to c.1890s, the way of life was completely different from that of today. Villages were almost self sufficient communities - in a way, they were mini republics, each jealously guarding its borders. The squire, usually the largest landowner, was the accepted leader of the community whose decisions were rarely questioned; he often provided land at a peppercorn rent for a community building, or some other recreational facility, gaining the respect of the community. Many of the houses in and around the village were owned by the squire, and most workers and their families lived in tied cottages. Farming provided the main source of employment, and the loss of one's job also meant the loss of the family home. The more wealthy farmers could afford to rent, from landowners, the farm with the best land, whilst those who were not so well off, rented the poor, and undrained land. Large areas of land in the Fylde were held by relatively few landlords - three examples are: (1) Lord Derby, with a vast estate including land at Weeton, Wharles, Treales and Inskip, (2) William Bashall who owned some 2,000 acres at Nateby, Pilling and Tarnacre, and (3) Thomas Horrocks Miller of Singleton.

Most large estates have now been "broken up", and sold. The face of the countryside itself has also changed as land is now more intensively cultivated. The old farm buildings are too small for modern tractors and combine harvesters, and many stone barns and old windmills have been converted into luxury homes. Very large farm buildings are required for modern machinery, to store hugh crops, and to house large herds of cattle. Milk quotas, 'set aside', and grain and beef "mountains" would have meant nothing to the grandfathers of the present farming community.

Traditional supportive industries have all but disappeared - the blacksmith, clogger (or shoemaker), farrier, saddler, tailor and wheelwright - all were common in almost every village at the beginning of the 20th century.

The village shopkeeper is finding it difficult to compete with present day supermarkets, and many 'corner shops' have closed. However, the distinctive aroma of ground coffee, the sight of open sacks of flour and spices, home cured hams hanging from the ceiling, and farmhouse butter and cheese in an old fashioned grocer's shop will no doubt evoke memories for many readers.

ALBERT CLAYTON'S

Above: *GARSTANG, Church Street, c.1890:* **Photograph by H. Jackson of Cleckheaton. A fine view of Church street looking east towards the Market Place. The Brown Cow Inn, which had the date 1685 and the initials 'C.G.E.' engraved on a lintel over the front door, is seen in the centre of the picture. In 1852, the landlord of the Brown Cow Inn, Septimus Smith, skilfully carved a watch chain, with a watch case at one end and a snuff box at the other, out of one solid piece of a broken gun-stock; every link in the chain was separate and it was admired for many years. The inn also housed a collection of counterfeit coins (it was a hanging offence in the early 19th century to pass counterfeit coins), and by c.1907 the Brown Cow Inn had become a small grocery shop and a farm house - the occupants being Jack Lawrenson and his wife who kept a few cows and hens in a field in Moss Lane which is now used as the playing field. The inn and the adjoining mill were demolished around the late 1920s, but the road at this point is still known by old Garstonians as 'Brown Cow Corner'.**

During the 19th century, it was common for a vicar to remain in the same parish for over 50 years. churches were well attended, and Sunday schools played an essential part in the upbringing and education of children; it was often necessary for vicars to require the assistance of a curate. As the 21st century approaches, many parishes have to share a vicar with two, or even three other parishes because of the decline in church attendance.

Doctors also tended to remain in the district for many years - only retiring when they became too aged or infirm to continue. It was common for doctors to travel round the district by horse and trap calling on up to 30 patients in a day. Desperately sick and poor people often received medical treatment without payment, although patients who were considered "better off" sometimes paid the doctor by trading off a piece of silver, or an item of furniture.

The motor car was in its infancy when the photographs were taken. Petrol was sold in two-gallon cans, and was obtainable at public houses, grocers' shops, cycle and hardware stores, and at tea rooms. Moses Holmes of Preesall Park Garage, stored petrol in open topped 40 gallon drums until he brought the first petrol pump to Preesall in 1926. Mr Holmes's son Tom, now aged 85 years, informed me that they used to ladle petrol out of the 40 gallon drum by using a gallon container. "It's a miracle that the place did not explode," he said.

The schoolmaster, and the policeman were the authoritative figures of village society. The village policeman was known to everyone and his administration of 'instant justice' prevented many a Court appearance. The laughter of children in the school playground remains the same, but the indoor games played by their forebears have been superseded - computers and electronic games now dominate.

Many of the old whitewashed, thatched cottages portrayed in this book have been demolished. The footscraper at the cottage door, the sight of a water pump (or well) in the garden, flagged floors, and the tin bath in front of the fire, are all in the past. The long hours of toil in the fields, or in the mills, for men women and children, are now all but forgotten. Children are better educated and their parents are no longer forced to work long hours in order to obtain a minimum standard of living. I have included a number of photographs of the town of Preston, although it is not a part of the Fylde. However, Preston markets have been an important link with the commerce of our Fylde villages for many generations. I feel privileged to share these nostalgic photographs and memories of the past with you. I trust you will obtain as much pleasure in reading 'Forgotten Fylde' as I have had in compiling it.

Albert J. Clayton,
St. Michael's on Wyre.
November 1995

Garstang & Barnacre with Bonds

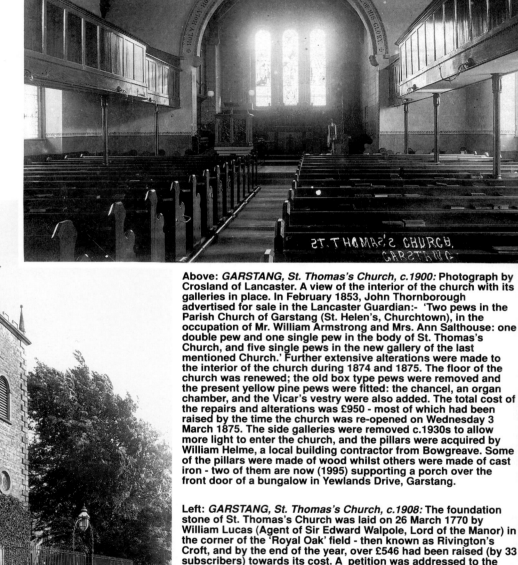

Above: *GARSTANG, St. Thomas's Church, c.1900:* Photograph by Crosland of Lancaster. A view of the interior of the church with its galleries in place. In February 1853, John Thornborough advertised for sale in the Lancaster Guardian:- 'Two pews in the Parish Church of Garstang (St. Helen's, Churchtown), in the occupation of Mr. William Armstrong and Mrs. Ann Salthouse: one double pew and one single pew in the body of St. Thomas's Church, and five single pews in the new gallery of the last mentioned Church.' Further extensive alterations were made to the interior of the church during 1874 and 1875. The floor of the church was renewed; the old box type pews were removed and the present yellow pine pews were fitted: the chancel, an organ chamber, and the Vicar's vestry were also added. The total cost of the repairs and alterations was £950 - most of which had been raised by the time the church was re-opened on Wednesday 3 March 1875. The side galleries were removed c.1930s to allow more light to enter the church, and the pillars were acquired by William Helme, a local building contractor from Bowgreave. Some of the pillars were made of wood whilst others were made of cast iron - two of them are now (1995) supporting a porch over the front door of a bungalow in Yewlands Drive, Garstang.

Left: *GARSTANG, St. Thomas's Church, c.1908:* The foundation stone of St. Thomas's Church was laid on 26 March 1770 by William Lucas (Agent of Sir Edward Walpole, Lord of the Manor) in the corner of the 'Royal Oak' field - then known as Rivington's Croft, and by the end of the year, over £546 had been raised (by 33 subscribers) towards its cost. A petition was addressed to the Bishop of Chester requesting that he should consecrate the new church by the title of 'All Saints'. The Rev James Pedder (Vicar of St. Helen's, Churchtown, the then Parish Church of Garstang) conducted the inaugural Divine Service on Sunday 7 December 1770. The year 1847 saw extensive repairs; the erection of the north gallery; the raising of the tower; the addition of ornamental battlements, and the gift of a burial ground by F. Walpole Keppel Esq. The church was eventually consecrated on 28 December 1848 in the name of St. Thomas. The road known as Chapel Street was then renamed Church Street. In 1880 an ecclesiastical district was assigned to St. Thomas's, Garstang which became the title of a separate parish. The Rev. George Boys Stones, who had been Curate in 1878, became its first Vicar until his retirement in 1914 - he died in 1923.

Right: *GARSTANG, The Fire Brigade, c.1890s:* Steam operated fire engines were first introduced c.1858, but it is not known when Garstang acquired the engine in the photograph. The firemen are seen at practice near the canal basin. On the evening of Friday 17 December 1897, a thatched house occupied by Mr. James Lea in Barnacre with Bonds, was discovered to be on fire. Mr. John Rawlinson, who was the captain of Garstang brigade, and Mr. John Nicholls were informed; they proceeded to the house where it was found that the source of the fire was near the chimney. The firemen removed some of the bricks from the chimney and poured water through the hole. After about an hour, it was thought that the fire had been extinguished, but at 11 p.m, Mrs. Lea was wakened by dense smoke in the bedroom; the alarm was raised and the volunteer brigade turned out in force. The firemen found that the roof timbers, and the thatched roof in close proximity to the chimney stack were blazing - the fire crew were successful in removing the burning thatch with fire hooks, and extinguishing the blaze, but not before considerable damage had been done. The house which had been rendered uninhabitable was situated across the road, mid way between the Church Inn and Saints Mary and Michael R.C. Church in Bonds.

Above: *GARSTANG, The Royal Oak Hotel, 1905:* At this time, the sight of a motor car was still a comparatively rare occurrence in Garstang. The public, who were inclined to the old horse drawn form of transport, were becoming increasingly alarmed by the choking dust being thrown up in the wake of these motorised vehicles. A traffic census was carried out in Garstang in 1911, at which time some 307 'mechanically propelled vehicles' travelled through the town each day: 1923 saw this number increase to 1,214; and by 1928 some 3,400 vehicles per day created serious traffic problems in the narrow streets of the town. The difficulties were alleviated on Monday 22 October 1928 when Garstang's by-pass road was officially opened.

MARKET PLACE, GARSTANG.

Above: *GARSTANG, High Street, c.1908:* Thomas's chemist's shop seen on the right of the photograph exists today, although it has been extensively modernised. The shop is situated almost across the road from the Town Hall which was built in 1755. The motor car on the left carried an early West Riding registration number C 1417. In January 1852, Garstang was created a Petty Sessions Division of the High Court. The first case to be heard was that of Benjamin Preston of Pilling, who was fined 5 shillings for poaching; this punishment contrasts sharply with that suffered by a Scotsman 14 years earlier. On 16 June 1838, John Chambers broke a shop window in Garstang, and stole about 50 silk and cotton handkerchiefs belonging to Alice Walmsley, a dressmaker: two days later, Chambers was discovered selling the items at considerably less than the 'marked up price'. The goods were recognised by Alice Walmsley who claimed that she had written the prices on the tickets attached to them. Chambers claimed that he had bought the goods from some pedlars who were travelling to Cockerham Fair; he was tried at the Midsummer Sessions at Preston. After hearing the evidence, the Jury deliberated 'for a few moments' and found the prisoner "Guilty" - he was sentenced to be "transported across the seas for a term of 7 years".

Right: *GARSTANG, R.W.Lang's Garage and Cycle repair depot c.1908:* A rare interior view of Richard William Lang's motor and cycle repair works which was situated in premises adjoining his home (Ivy Cottage) on Bridge Street; he later acquired additional premises directly across the street from his home. Mr Lang also operated a well known painting, decorating and plumbing business. The building in the photograph exists today.

R.W. LANG, CYCLE & MOTOR WORKS, GARSTANG, R.S.O.

8

GARSTANG, William Crozier's Newsagent's Shop, Stoops Hall, mid 1920s: **After William (Billy) Crozier's death, the business was run by his daughter and son-in-law - Dorothy and Ben Longworth, two of Garstang's best known characters. The Croziers were an old Garstang family, some of whose members had previously been Garstang's town criers.**

ELLEL, Bay Horse Station, c.1905: Photograph by George Howarth of Lancaster. When the Preston Junction to Lancaster railway was opened in 1840, Bay Horse Station was one of the original stations although it is likely that the buildings in the picture were built some time after that date. A serious accident occurred here on Monday 21 August 1848 when a northbound express ran into the rear of a stationary local train. The rear two carriages of the stationary train were completely demolished; one person, 43 year old Hannah Airey, was killed and a number of butchers from Preston, who were travelling to Hornby Fair, were badly injured. The station closed for passenger traffic on 13 June 1960, but the station continued to be used for goods traffic until 16 May 1964; it has since been demolished although the station house remains.

BONDS near GARSTANG, The Church Inn, c.1892: Photograph by Herbert Jackson of Cleckheaton. Saints Mary and Michael R.C. Church (built 1857/8) can be seen in the background. The inn was formerly known as the 'Rose and Crown Inn' until the church was built and its name was changed to the Church Inn. The date stone over the front door (now bricked up) reads 1753. Today, between the church and the inn, there are two pairs of semi detached houses which were built c.1894/5 which dates this photograph before that time. Many of Jackson's photographs were printed as postcards at the height of the postcard boom in 1904, although many of the photographs had been taken up to 15 years earlier, and had been on sale throughout the 1890s as cabinet photographs.

ALBERT CLAYTON'S

BARNACRE, Sandholme Mill Cottage, 1899: Photograph by Crosland of Lancaster. One of the Fylde's most heart rending tragedies took place in this wayside cottage. Mary Annie (Polly) Simpson can be seen on the right of the photograph. On Whit-Tuesday 1901, whilst suffering from severe depression, Mary Annie drowned her three children in a Dolly tub; she was taken in custody to Lancaster Assizes where she was found unfit to plead, and spent a number of years in Lancaster Asylum. The names of the three children were Annie aged 4 years and 9 months; Florence aged 3 years and 3 months, and Allan Edwin aged 3 months; the two oldest children are also in the photograph. The cottage became the venue for thousands of sightseers; it has been demolished for many years, although the site is clearly identifiable and some brickwork remains. The miller at Sandholme Mill at the time was Thomas Smith.

BARNACRE, GARSTANG & CATTERALL STATION, June 1911: In June 1911, Garstang was invaded by around 15,000 Territorial Army personnel who arrived at Garstang and Catterall Station, and were housed in tents in what became known as Claughton Camp. The troops were extremely well organised. Support units included the Medical Corps, the Royal Field Artillery, the Service Corps, the Engineers, and even a Post Office. A mock invasion of the area was staged with the 5th to 8th Battalions of the Manchester Regiment comprising the White force, and the Lancashire Fusileers comprising the Brown force. The area covered by the invasion included Dolphinholme, Scorton, Nateby, Claughton, Barnacre and as far away as Clitheroe. The main 'battle' took place on Friday and Saturday 16 and 17 June 1911. The only casualty (with over 500 Medical Corps men available) was a broken leg, sustained by one of the Engineers who had been kicked by a horse. The soldiers are seen arriving on the northbound platform.

BARNACRE, GARSTANG & CATTERALL STATION, June 1911: Soldiers of the 8th Manchester Regiment marching past the Kenlis Arms Hotel (out of view to the right of the photograph), having arrived at the station in preparation for the massive Military exercise which was about to take place. Note the photographer in the field to the left of the picture.

BARNACRE WITH BONDS, Bowgreave Police Station, c.1909: The police station was built 1855/6 on Bowgreave Hill at a cost of £1300. It was the first building to be built on the summit, although there were other houses lower down the hill towards Catterall. Inside the police station there was originally a metal spiral staircase to the right of the front door; there was accomodation for prisoners, who enjoyed the warmth of a coal fire outside two cells, and there was a mortuary in a cellar below the level of the office floor (the ground slopes steeply away from the front of the building). The cellar has been filled in and the mortuary slab is now used at the rear of the building as part of a path. The windows to the left of the office formed part of the house where the superintendent or chief inspector lived. The view has changed little over the years - even the Victorian letter box has survived. The police station in Garstang was formerly situated at the rear of the Town Hall, and the town constable lived in a house at 60 Bridge Street.

ALBERT CLAYTON'S

SECTION 2
South of Garstang

CLAUGHTON, Old Claughton Garage, c.1930: In 1923, Lancashire County Council conducted a traffic census at Claughton toll bar and at Snapewood bridge at Cabus. In 1924, L.C.C. decided to build a new road to by-pass the town of Garstang. The shopkeepers in the town complained that they would lose business as a result, but when it was explained to them that all the buildings on the east side of town would have to be demolished if the new road was to be built through the town, the objections ceased. The preliminary work in marking out the route of the by-pass began in November 1925. The work was estimated to cost £96,000 with a Ministry of Transport grant of 75%, and was carried out by Sir Lindsay Parkinson & Co, of Blackpool and Messrs. Turners of Manchester, employing mainly Irish labourers. Nicholas Bamber, the owner of Claughton Garage, which was situated between the Brockholes Arms Hotel and the old Claughton toll bar, quickly realised the adverse effect that the new road would have on his business, and he purchased a plot of land further south on the east side of the A6 trunk road, at the junction with New Lane. In 1927 Mr. Bamber built a new garage (also known as Claughton Garage), and his old premises were taken over by Reg Slater who lived at Boyes Cottage, Catterall. Mr. Slater made hen cabins and sold poultry appliances. A hand operated petrol pump can be seen in the photograph. The premises were later acquired by the firm of Hesfords who sold and repaired agricultural implements. The by-pass was officially opened by Sir Henry Maybury, Director General of Roads, on Monday 22 October 1928.

The Hall

CLAUGHTON.

CLAUGHTON, Claughton Hall, c.1900: Photograph by H. Jackson of Cleckheaton. Claughton Hall as seen in the photograph was partly re-built in 1816/17 by William Fitzherbert-Brockholes on the site of the old Hall, part of which had been burnt down towards the end of the 18th century. William, who lived at Mains Hall, near Poulton, moved to Claughton where he lived for only a short time before he died, leaving the estate to Thomas, his eldest son. Thomas, a batchelor, lived here for 60 years and was probably responsible for much of the landscaping carried out on the estate. At the beginning of World War II the Hall was taken over by the Ministry of Health - it was later occupied by Nuns and children from Patricroft, Manchester. It was then let for around 8 years to 'The White Fathers', - a Roman Catholic Order - for the purpose of re-training Priests for Ministry in the Colonies. The Hall reverted back to the Fitzherbert-Brockholes family, and a firm of independent architects was commissioned to carry out a survey of the building. The survey concluded that the Hall could not be restored into a satisfactory dwelling house, and in 1957 the Hall was demolished. The present Hall was built on the same site, and in October 1958 it was occupied by Mr. Michael J.Fitzherbert-Brockholes and his family.

14

ALBERT CLAYTON'S

CLAUGHTON, Fishers, Bowman Cottage, c.1906: The Fisher family farmed here in the early 20th century until c.1913. The farm was approximately 10 acres in extent and formed part of the estate of the Fitzherbert-Brockholes family. Thomas Fisher and later Matthew Fisher, also carried on business as shoemakers, but by the time Charlie Winder had become the tenant of nearby Bowman farm in 1934, the old cottage had become derelict - the thatched roof had collapsed and the bedroom floor was in a precarious condition. Access to the bedrooms was gained by climbing stone steps inside the cottage. The ruins of the walls were finally levelled in April 1995 although a small section of the left hand gable wall remains - this is used as a 'fence' for horse jumping. The cobbled paths and the foundations of the old cottage are still clearly visible (1995). The wood at the rear of the cottage is known as Bowman wood.

BROCK, The Green Man Inn, c.1906: The Green Man Inn was once a busy coaching station. The public house is said to be almost 400 years old - soldiers were provided with refreshments during the Civil War (c.1644), and Scottish troops were entertained on their way south during the 1745 Rebellion.

BROCK, c.1904: The cottage in the photograph was a well known landmark for over 200 years, being situated at the side of the main road between Preston and Garstang at a point some 50 yards north of Brock bridge; it is believed that the cottage was built from cobbles which had been obtained from the nearby River Brock. In 1907, the cottage was owned by Thomas Holmes who had 9 children, all of whom were brought up here. Water for washing was obtained from the River Brock, whilst drinking water was pumped from a well (out of the picture to the left of the cottage). The lane on the right leads to Brock railway station. When Thomas Holmes came here he opened a hardware store and shop in a lean to at the rear of the premises - and also provided teas in the orchard for passing cyclists and travellers. Mrs Holmes was kept very busy washing (using plenty of 'elbow grease', starch and dolly blue), ironing, darning socks, knitting, and attending to the needs of a large family, besides running a shop and making teas. Baking was done in a fireside oven, and candles were initially used for lighting (anyone with a paraffin lamp was considered to be 'well off'). In July 1990 the cottage was demolished.

BROCK, The Railway Station, c.1905: Photograph by A. Stott. A view looking south towards Preston, showing Bilsborrow Lane bridge in the distance which was the site of the original Roebuck station before the station was moved to this location c.1840s. Behind the stationmaster's house on the left of the photograph, there used to be a row of four railway cottages known as Parlick Terrace. On 29 May 1920, and again in January 1954, Parlick Terrace was flooded to a depth of over 2 feet by the overflowing of the nearby River Brock. The station buildings, platforms and Parlick Terrace have been demolished - only the pedestrian crossing remains. Brock station closed for passengers on 1 May 1939, but remained open for goods until 5 April 1954 although coal was supplied to a coal merchant for some time later.

BROCK, *Matshead Mill, c.1904/5:* A view of the old paper mill - which has now been demolished and the mill pond filled in. It was owned by the Bateson family and was situated at the side of the River Brock, approximately quarter of a mile upstream from Brock station. The Bateson family made brown wrapping paper which was transported by road to Liverpool until the coming of the railway in 1840.

BILSBORROW/MYERSCOUGH, *c.1907:* The view is still recognisable despite extensive alterations to the road, and to the Roebuck Inn. The road was considerably widened in 1923 and again in 1931, at which time the County Council Baccus bridge (in right distance) was also removed and set back to the right, on the side of what is now part of the Roebuck Inn car park. The lane in the left foreground used to lead to the Roebuck canal bridge - which was approached by a dangerous bend in the road. The old canal bridge was replaced by the present bridge which was built during 1969/70.

MYERSCOUGH, White Horse Village, c.1912: **Photograph by A.E.Shaw of Blackburn. The White Horse Inn (to the centre right) was the scene of a conspiracy in November 1803 to rob Thomas and John Eccles, two elderly brothers who lived at Fell End Farm, Oakenclough. Three villains named Henry Barker, James Chadwick, and Jonas Clark from Manchester, were seen talking to Richard Eccles, a nephew of the Eccles brothers in the White Horse Inn. Eccles was later seen walking towards Oakenclough in the company of the villains. Shortly afterwards, during the night of 30 November, the Eccles brothers were awakened in their bedroom by intruders with blackened faces - the elder brother was violently assaulted and robbed of a considerable amount of gold (£200 - £300). The perpetrators were arrested in Manchester, and sent for trial at Lancaster Assizes - Jonas Clark turned 'King's evidence' and he and Richard Eccles (insufficient evidence against him) were acquitted, but Chadwick and Barker were publicly executed at Lancaster on 28 April 1804 by 'Ned' Barlow, the most hated man in Lancaster at the time. Ned, a Welshman, was executioner from 1782 to 1835.**

BARTON, Station Lane and Newhouse R.C. Church: c.1905: **Photograph by Frederick Cooper of Preston. A Roman Catholic mission was founded here c.1730, and the original building was replaced in 1805 by the church seen on the left of the photograph: in 1906, this church was pulled down and the present church was built.**

BARTON, Barton Hall, c.1905: Photograph by G. Cross. Barton Hall was formerly known as Barton Lodge, and was the home of the Jacson (sic) family from c.1834. Following the death of Charles Roger Jacson in 1893, the Barton Hall estate was offered for sale at £104,000, but no purchaser was found. In June 1899, the trustees divided the estate into 72 separate lots and it was sold by auction. The Hall was requisitioned by the Royal Air Force during World War II, and later became an Air Traffic Control Centre; it was demolished c.1980s and the site is now used as an Animal Health Centre. A private small whitewashed chapel was formerly attached to the estate; this chapel was consecrated the Church of St. Lawrence on the 9 October 1850. The old building was pulled down c.1895 and the present church was built; it was consecrated in July 1896.

BARTON & BROUGHTON, The Railway Station, c.1904: In August 1839, before the Preston Junction/Lancaster railway had been completed, it was decided to build 3 intermediate stations - one near the Bay Horse Hotel in Ellel, one in Ray Lane near Garstang, and another near the Roebuck Inn at Bilsborrow. Some 6 months later, the number of stations was increased to six - the additional stations being at Galgate, Scorton and Crow Hall, near Barton. Originally Scorton and Crow Hall were small 'sentry boxes' with few facilities, but they were later replaced, and more substantial platforms and buildings were erected when the original 'stations' were moved to new locations. The view of Barton & Broughton station looks south towards Preston. Further north, the line between White Horse bridge and Bilsborrow Lane bridge was originally a single track, and goods trains often had to wait at the original Roebuck station for other trains to overtake. Shortly before the railway was opened, and again on Tuesday 7 July 1840, (only 12 days after the railway was opened) White Horse railway bridge, which is situated approximately 1 mile to the north of Broughton station, collapsed.

BROUGHTON, The Cross Roads, c.1910: A familiar scene at one of the busiest cross roads in the Fylde. Note the Automobile Association sign on the side of the Golden Ball Hotel. The AA copied the idea of recommending hotels or inns from the Cyclists' Touring Club (C.T.C.) who had been recommending inns to their members before the turn of the century. Fylde innkeepers had suffered greatly since the 1840s when the railways appeared, and ruined the stage coach and post-chaise traffic: what a devastating impact this must have had! The busy clatter of horses' hooves in the stable yards, the services of the ostlers, the staff at the inns - all went as the passing trade declined. Thereafter, the roadside inns had to rely on local trade, or the chance custom of a passing commercial traveller, known then as a bagman. What a boon it must have been to the old inns when the motor car arrived on the scene, and the customers began to return in ever increasing numbers.

BROUGHTON, Richard Hardman's Joiner's Shop, c.1905: Photograph by G. Cross. The house on the left of the photograph is still in existence, being situated near to the old toll house. The joiner's shop no longer exists, and the area now forms part of King George's playing fields. One of the carts in the picture belonged to William Price of Cross House Dairy.

ALBERT CLAYTON'S

BROUGHTON, The Parish Church of St. John the Baptist, c.1900: Photograph by Arthur Winter of Preston. The church is seen before the extensive alterations which were carried out in 1904 when a chancel and side vestries were added. The body of the church was built c.1826, replacing a church which dated back to the beginning of the 16th century. The tower bears the date 1533 and this is thought to be the date of its construction. Anthony Hewitson, in his book Northward, states that there was a church in existence here in the year 1112.

GOOSNARGH, Blake Hall, c.1908: One of the Fylde's historic and secluded farm houses that has changed little over the centuries. Since the photograph was taken, the door has been moved to where the small window and water butt are situated - apart from this, it remains substantially the same. The house is thought to date from the early 17th century, and the rooms are supported by massive dark oak beams. Thomas Whittaker, one of the Roman Catholic Martyrs, was captured here (at Midgall's, Blake Hall) in August 1643; he was imprisoned in Lancaster Castle where he was executed on 7 August 1646. The unfortunate soul was forced to watch as two other Priests were hung, drawn and quartered, before he too suffered the same dreadful fate. The lady standing in the doorway is Mrs. Mary Lancaster, whose husband Richard farmed here. In 1929, an oak refectory table, and a bench with a panelled back, both of which were dated 1630 and bore the initials of the Midgall family, were removed from Blake Hall, and sold by E.J.Reed of Preston.

GOOSNARGH, *The Village, c.1909:* A fine animated photograph of Goosnargh with the tower of the ancient church of St. Mary visible in the background. In September 1838, Goosnargh churchyard was packed with an estimated 2,000 people who witnessed the burial of Ann Sanderson and her 5 children (of Fairhurst Cottage, Inglewhite), whom she had poisoned with arsenic. The top of the tower was packed to capacity, and every available space in the churchyard was occupied, as Ann and her children were buried side by side on the north side of the church. The children's coffins were draped in white linen, whilst their mother's was draped in black. The site of the graves was originally marked by a mound of earth, but this has been levelled out and the exact position is not known.

GOOSNARGH, *The Corn Mill, c.1910:* The water powered Corn Mill was leased by John Procter in 1900 for a term of 7 years, and in 1907 he bought the mill and several closes of land. The mill remained in the Procter family until 1962 when it was sold to Ribble Feeds Ltd. The age of the mill is uncertain. The mill house has the date 1722 carved on a lintel, but it is likely that there has been a water powered corn mill on or near this site for many generations before that date. In the photograph are, left to right: John Procter, Tim Procter (of Chipping Mill), Molly and Maggie Procter (John's children), and standing in the doorway is a person who was affectionately known as 'Long Tom'.

ALBERT CLAYTON'S

THE BAND, WHITTINGHAM ASYLUM

WHITTINGHAM, The Asylum Band, c.1906/7: A photograph taken by A.E.Shaw of Blackburn of an impressive group of musicians at Whittingham Asylum. I believe they would be more suitably described as an orchestra rather than a band. At this time, anyone who could play a musical instrument, or who was a good cricketer, would be assured of employment at the Asylum! A present day estimate of the value of the instruments must be close to £100,000. The Asylum opened on 1 April 1873, and between 1873 and 1895, approximately 1500 patients were buried in Goosnargh churchyard - often as many as eight coffins deep. The Asylum closed on 31 March 1995.

SECTION 3
Preston

PRESTON, The Butter and Egg Market, c.1905: Photograph by Frederick Cooper, North Road, Preston. The market was held outside the old Corn Exchange (The Public Hall). The Corporation Arms public house at the corner of Wharf Street and Lune Street, can be seen on the right of the picture. A dreadful accident occurred here on Monday 3 October 1853 during the cotton weavers and spinners lock out and strike. The landlord of the Corporation Arms had allowed the relief committee to pay out hardship money to those who were badly affected by the prolonged dispute, from a room above the coach house. Access to the room was gained by climbing 16 stone steps on the outside of the building. The room was crowded with around 200 persons when the large beam which supported the floor gave way, and the occupants cascaded onto each other into the coach house below as the floor assumed a 'V' shape. Many people received broken limbs and one girl (Jane Smalley, aged 13 years, a card room hand at Ainsworth's Mill) was killed, adding to the misery already being suffered by the people of Preston as a result of the dispute. It was later discovered that there was a large knot in the beam where it had given way. An inquest was held in the Town Hall on Wednesday 5 October, when the jury returned a verdict of "Accidental Death".

PRESTON, The Virgin's Inn, c.1890: The Virgin's Inn was the last thatched house in the centre of old Preston, and was situated in Anchor Weind, nearly opposite the entrance to Anchor Court, and occupied a site close to the south west corner of the present main Post Office, near the junction of Market Street and the Market Place. The premises were demolished in February 1894. At the time of its demolition there was a search for 'treasure trove', but only a few old coins were found. The demolition was part of the scheme to clear all the ancient property from the north side of the old Market Place, as far as the present covered market.

PRESTON, Fishergate Hill, c.1912: Photograph by A.E. Shaw of Blackburn. A scene to conjure with as tramcar No. 22 travels up Fishergate Hill towards the town centre. County Hall is seen in the centre of the photograph. The three storey buildings to the left of the tramcar have been demolished and the land now forms part of the County Hall complex.

FORGOTTEN FYLDE ALBUM

PRESTON, Shoeing Forge, 1905: Thomas Wallis, 72 Higher Bank Road, Preston, at work at his shoeing forge. Large numbers of blacksmiths were employed shoeing horses in towns, as well as in the country. The London Midland and Scottish Railway Co. (L.M.S.) for instance, had around 40/50 'geldings' (these were known as 'grafters'), which delivered goods in carts round Preston. The horses were housed in stables on Christian Road, and a chain horse was often required to assist the gelding to pull its heavily laden cart up the steep incline in the road. Traffic on Fishergate Hill was often halted in order to allow the horses to emerge onto the main road. I remember (c.1949) seeing, as I waited for a Viking bus, one L.M.S. horse slipping onto its knees on the granite setts outside the firm of Gascoignes in Starchhouse Square. The cart was so overloaded that the poor animal had great difficulty in moving it. I vividly recall the horse receiving unmerciful encouragement from the driver, as it struggled in its attempt to regain its feet.

PRESTON, The Market Place, c.1904: The covered market on the right of the photograph was completed c.1875. According to the Rev. Richard Warner in his book published in 1803 entitled "A tour through the Northern Counties of England and the Borders of Scotland," the market regulations in force in 1803 were as follows: "The time of selling begins at 8 a.m. from which time, till 9 a.m. no person, unless he is an inhabitant of Preston, can purchase any article exposed for sale. From 9 a.m. everything is sold indiscriminately until 1 p.m. when the Market closes, and before which nothing is allowed to be withdrawn from the stalls, except fish, which can be carried away in panniers as soon as the town is supplied." At that time, the area in the photograph was an Orchard. Markets of one sort or another used to be held every day in Preston. The Monday market was given over to drapery and millinery, whilst the markets on Tuesday and Thursday were for the sale of hay and straw. On Wednesdays and Fridays the market was for general produce. Friday used to be the main market day, but by 1904, Saturday had become the great market day when farmers, laden with their produce, gathered outside the Public Hall.

PRESTON, The Preston Industrial Co-operative Society, 1906: **The Grocery and Butchers' departments at 157 & 159 St. George's Road were opened c.1875. The road on the extreme left is St. Paul's Road. The notices on the wall advertise a quarterly meeting of the Society in St. Paul's schoolroom, Pole Street, on Monday 8 October 1906.**

PRESTON, Dredger No. 9 leaving Preston Dock c.1910: **The suction hopper dredger is seen leaving Preston Dock and was photographed from the 'Bull-nose' - a popular vantage point for photographers. The dredger was built by Ferguson Brothers Ltd., of Glasgow in 1907, and was sold in 1927 to J.G.Mouritzen & Co., of Copenhagen who renamed it *Suomi*.**

PRESTON, The wreckage of the Scottish Express, 1896: At 12.16 a.m. on Monday 13 July, the down Scottish sleeping car express (known as the "Tourist's Express"), passed through Preston Station, double headed by the engines *Shark* and *Vulcan*. The drivers, anxious to keep to a tight time schedule between Preston and Carlisle, ignored the 10 m.p.h. speed limit which was in force, and passed through at an estimated 40 m.p.h. Just north of the station, the leading engine (*Shark*) jumped the 'V' shaped points on a tight left hand curve, and ploughed straight on into a broad siding, coming to rest within a few feet of a 20 foot drop into Stevenson's Iron Foundry. The 2 sleeping carriages, 4 ordinary carriages and the guard's van were badly damaged, and wreckage was scattered over a wide area. The train had 16 passengers on board; one was killed and 9 people (including both drivers) were injured. An inquest was held on Tuesday 21 July; one of the jury members was Arthur Winter, who took the photograph. The jury returned a verdict of "Accidental Death".

ALBERT CLAYTON'S

PRESTON, Atkinson's Livery Stables, 30 Waterloo Road, c.1900: A splendid cabinet photograph of one of John Atkinson's covered landaus. John Atkinson was in business as a cab proprietor for over 35 years, firstly at Elm Villas, Waterloo Terrace, and later at 30 Waterloo Road, Ashton.

PRESTON, Tramcar No. 12 at Moor Park entrance gates on Garstang Road, c.1904/5. On Tuesday 7 June 1904, Preston Corporation replaced the old horse drawn tramcars with an electric tramway system. The new electric tramcars were made by the firm of Dick, Kerr's in Strand Road, Preston.

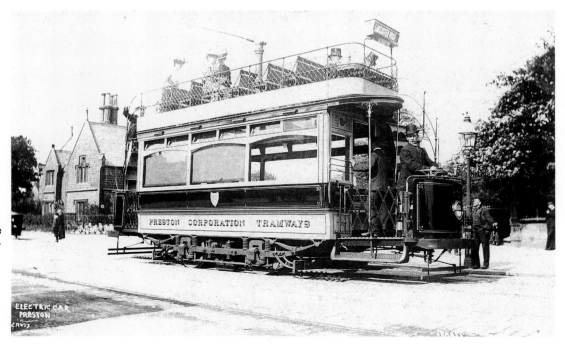

SECTION 4
Central Fylde

CHURCHTOWN I

CHURCHTOWN, The Green, c.1890s: Photograph by Crosland of Lancaster. A fine view showing The Horns Inn on the left of the picture with a thatched cottage beyond (demolished c.1900). In July 1929, Lancashire County Council proposed to move Churchtown's ancient Cross - demolish the adjacent Manor Cottages, and route the main road straight through the village. The intended scheme caused a great deal of concern amongst the residents. The Rev. J.C.Hood, the Vicar of St. Helen's Church, was elected spokesman for the residents to oppose this proposed act of 'vandalism' - the scheme was subsequently altered and the present by-pass was built c.193 which diverted the traffic round the village.

CHURCHTOWN, 1923: A dignified funeral cortege at St. Helen's Church on a rainy day in 1923. Local undertakers made coffins, and their wives or daughters often made the shrouds. The undertakers occasionally missed getting paid for a funeral because the family was too poor, but in many Fylde villages, Friendly Societies were established. On payment of a few pence each week, a sum was given on the death of a member (usually around £10) which covered the cost of the funeral. A coffin made of oak cost around £1 more than one made of beech or ash. Where the church was situated close to the home of the deceased, a hearse was not used. Members of the family or neighbours, in turn, carried the coffin to church, changing over at regular intervals. An interesting article appeared in the "London Globe" on 22 February 1811:- "Death - on Sunday week, aged 70 - the eccentric Tom Brown of Garstang. Tom was an occasional useful assistant in the kitchens of the neighbouring gentry; he could either 'please the taste' or 'mend a sole' with any man of his day, but Tom would neither make nor mend with the Lords of Creation (women); though he lived by himself and washed, cooked, made and mended for himself, he would only take the measure of a female's foot: this partiality continued till his death. A short time prior to his death, he selected 36 female acquaintances to attend his funeral, all of whom attended, and were regaled at Mr. Henry Woodworth's of Churchtown with coffee and tea. He also ordered every child in the town a penny loaf, which was given accordingly, and he has left all his property among his female relatives."

30

CHURCHTOWN, Church Street, c.1904: Photograph by H. Jackson of Cleckheaton. In one of the whitewashed cottages on the left of the picture (behind the trees), lived Ann Maria Helme, who lived to be 103 years of age: her age was unknown until she died at the home of her niece Janet Bamber, in Church Street, Churchtown on the afternoon of Wednesday 16 May 1923; she outlived her husband by 22 years. It was only after her husband's death in 1901 that she began to 'stand' Garstang Market, and became famous at the market for the 'lively banter' which she carried on with her customers who constantly teased her about her high prices, but she always gave more than she received: Ann's family went to Churchtown in the mid 19th century where her father worked for the Rev. Wilson Pedder (Vicar from 1855 until his death in 1891): she was twice married - her second husband being Robert Helme, a shoemaker from St. Michael's who later became a gamekeeper on the Kirkland Hall estate. The cottages on the left behind the trees have been demolished, and the land forms part of the Punch Bowl Inn car park. Note the brickwork on the gable end of the Punch Bowl Inn (to the centre right of the photograph). It appears that the roof has been raised on two occasions, and it is possible that this was originally a single storey property.

CHURCHTOWN, Whitsuntide Procession, Whit -Tuesday, 9 June 1908: Churchtown and Garstang formerly held their Whitsuntide processions on Whit Monday in alternate years, but Garstang decided to hold them annually - thus creating some ill feeling between them. However, the problem was resolved when Churchtown decided to hold their procession on Whit Tuesday - a day when Calder Vale also held their festival. On this glorious sunny day in 1908, the procession is seen assembling in The Avenue before wending its way to the Parish Church of St. Helen's.

CHURCHTOWN, The Cross, c.1895: A view of this familiar landmark which has changed little over the years. The lady in the doorway of her home (Manor Cottages) on the right of the photograph is Hannah Hindle who died on 2 March 1899, aged 79 years. On 16 November 1816, Thomas Butler Cole of Kirkland Hall, nephew of the late Alexander Butler, came into possession of the estate when he celebrated his 21st birthday. Church bells were rung at an early hour and a sumptuous feast was given at the Hall for his many friends. Tenants were entertained at the local inns, and to each of his servants he gave a sum of money; his cottage tenants were each given a joint of beef, and a guinea. The festivities on the first day ended with a dance at the Hall: also on the first day of the festivities, which lasted all week, two men died. Thomas Cartmell died from suffocation by drinking to excess, and John Royle was found drowned in the River Wyre. However great the cost of this week of celebrations, it was nothing to the costs awarded against the young squire at Lancaster Assizes on 21 March 1818, when he was sued for breach of promise of marriage, and ordered to pay £7000 damages to Miss M. A. Orford, the daughter of an eminent Warrington surgeon. Thomas Butler Cole died in 1864 aged 68 years.

CATTERALL, Catterall Hall & Swing Bridge, c.1905:
The ancient Manor House of Catterall is said to date back to the 14th century. In 1704, the Manor House was bought by Thomas Winckley, a noted Preston lawyer, who pulled down the old structure, and replaced it with the farm house shown in the photograph. Many additions and alterations to its structure have taken place since that time. The present owner, during restoration work, has revealed a number of blocked up windows and doorways, and has discovered from the appearance of some of the timbers, lintels and beams which have been used in its construction, it is likely that they were taken from the ancient wooden Manor House. The barn, in the centre of the photograph, is dated 1839. The age of the swing bridge is uncertain - it was in existence before 1847 and was the subject of a letter from the Rev. Wilson Pedder to Garstang Highways Board on 6 April 1885, when he complained that the wooden bridge was in a

dangerous condition. The Highways Board decided that they were not obliged to repair it since they had no power beyond the fences of the highways. If they were to repair the bridge, they would be called upon to repair every other bridge in Garstang Union.

Left: *ST. MICHAEL'S on WYRE, c.1906:* 'Dick' Cooper from Gisburn came to St. Michael's every summer for about 20 years, and stayed at John Horn's Refreshment Rooms near the church. Dick made this his base as he went round the district trapping moles and fastening their dead bodies on nearby barbed wire fences which indicated to the farmer that he was doing his job - he found rich pickings on the soft peaty soil surrounding the village and on Tarnacre, Inskip and Rawcliffe mosses. The secret of being a successful mole catcher is that you must always leave a few, to allow them to breed; this ensures that you are called upon the following year! The photograph shows Dick with all his mole catching equipment (note his leather knee pad). The Fylde used to see many itinerent workers with widely differing skills. I remember 'Tar Jack' who went round tarring (and sleeping in) Dutch barns in the 1940/50s; his clothes were caked with a waterproof coating of tar and he worked well into old age: he was eventually found dead in a barn belonging to Mr. T. R. Sudell, of Clarkson Green Farm, in Catforth. Tramp tailors also used to travel up and down the country earning their money at their customary tailors' workshops, staying a few weeks before moving on to fresh pastures - only to return again the following year.

Below: *ST. MICHAEL'S on WYRE, The School, c.1912:* In 1806, the children were taught in an old whitewashed thatched cottage, situated at the junction of Rawcliffe Road and Garstang Road. The Headmaster at this time was Henry Fisher. In 1836, a new school was built by the Rev. Hugh Hornby, Vicar of St. Michael's, at his own expense, on land adjoining the churchyard. The school was condemned under the regulations laid down by the 1891 Education Act, and was replaced in 1893 by the one in the photograph, which was designed by James Jemson of Cockerham, and built at a cost of £816 14s 11d. It was situated at the junction of Hall Lane and Blackpool Road, and the photograph shows the Headmaster, Mr. John Moss leaning over the gate. John Moss went to St. Michael's in 1889 from Nostell Priory where he had been private tutor for 15 years to the Hon. Cecil Winn, the son of Lord St. Oswald, before which he was headmaster at Weeton school for 4 years. John Moss was an expert botanist, ornithologist, and an accomplished organist and composer who retired on 28 March 1918 after serving as headmaster for more than 28 years: he died in April 1925. The school was finally abandoned on Wednesday 22 October 1969, when the present school was opened. The school in the photograph was demolished c.1970, and two houses now occupy the site.

ST. MICHAEL'S on WYRE, The Grapes Hotel, c.1906: A photograph showing work in progress painting the sign above the front door. Robert J. Sumner went to the Grapes Hotel in 1902 and left in 1909 - to be replaced as landlord by Henry Huntington. On bonfire night 1863, Thomas Butler, the 18 year old son of the landlord of the Grapes Hotel - who was also the local joiner and wheelwright - accompanied by a number of his friends, decided to purchase some loose gunpowder from the ironmonger's shop in Garstang. The group of men went into a field to the rear of the Grapes Hotel (then known as the Black Bull Inn) near the River Wyre, where the gunpowder was placed inside the hub of a wagon wheel and both ends were sealed. Thomas Butler fitted a short fuse, and by using a lighted rag on the end of a fishing rod, he lit the fuse, and the young men took shelter behind the river bank. A loud explosion took place, and the hub was projected into the air. Butler decided to repeat the exercise - he went through the same procedure, but unfortunately for him, the fuse would not light so he looked over the top of the river bank, and watched as he applied the lighted torch to the hub which unknown to Butler, had been weakened by the previous explosion. The hub exploded without giving him time to seek shelter. A piece of the hub struck him on the head taking away a large part of his skull; he died before medical assistance could be summoned, and he was buried near the vestry on the north side of the parish church on 9 November 1863.

34

ALBERT CLAYTON'S

Above: *ST. MICHAEL'S on WYRE, c.1907:* Photograph by R.W.Lord of Poulton. A busy scene in St. Michael's with a group of visitors arriving by wagonette at Robinson's Tea Rooms (a house known as Wyre View), which was built by John Robinson in 1906. The house in the centre of the picture, built in 1877/8, was one of the village tailor's shops, and was owned by John Fisher Jnr, who specialised in making riding breeches and gamekeeper's jackets. Four generations of the Fisher family were tailors in St. Michael's for over 140 years. In August 1878, John Fisher was approached by the Garstang Board of Guardians to take Joseph Iddon, a 15 year old boy as an apprentice. Joseph lived at Nateby, and both his parents had died. It was the duty of the guardians to find employment for such young people, rather than allow them to become a charge upon the ratepayers. John Fisher agreed to take him for a period of 6 years. Mr Fisher had to agree to allow Joseph to attend the Church of England Sunday School, and Joseph had not to work more than 10 miles from St. Michael's. It was also the duty of the guardians to make periodic visits to the apprentices in order to assess their progress. On one visit, Joseph was asked if he had any complaints: he replied that he was getting too much fresh salmon to eat! John Fisher was a keen fisherman and there was a plentiful supply of salmon in the River Wyre at that time.

Below: *ST. MICHAEL'S on WYRE, The Village, 1906:* Photograph by A. E. Shaw of Blackburn. With the exception of the whitewashed cottage, the houses were built between 1800 and 1840. The whitewashed cottage nearest the camera was demolished in 1911, and a new reading room was built on the site in 1912. In 1905, a sparrow club was formed in St. Michael's - it was run on the lines suggested by the Board of Agriculture. The club consisted of honorary members (usually farmers and landowners), and working members, each paying a subscription on a sliding scale to a treasurer, who paid out 3d for every 6 old sparrows killed, or 3d for every 12 newly fledged sparrows killed, and 3d for every 24 eggs, all of which had to be killed or collected within two and a half miles of St. Michael's Church. The payments were made on a weekly basis, and prizes of 3 shillings and 2 shillings were made to the 2 most successful working members at the end of the year (funds permitting - rule 3). Strict rules were enforced - there had to be no trespassing on farmers' land. By December 1905, the club had a debit balance of 6 shillings and 10 pence. Sparrows were considered to be a menace by farmers, and as late as 1921, Garstang Rural District Council made payments to 5 parish councils for dead birds.

Above: *ST. MICHAEL'S on WYRE, The Egg collectors, c.1915:* On 10 December 1914, the War Office decided to implement a nationwide scheme for the weekly collection of 200,000 eggs to be consumed by wounded soldiers and sailors (the Royal Flying Corps had not then been formed). The eggs were initially sent to London, but as the numbers of wounded increased, the eggs were sent to local hospitals. Some 78 collecting districts were established throughout the country. The scheme quickly got under way in all the townships in Garstang Union. The collectors were each given a Red Cross badge and went round their townships in all weathers - sometimes accepting money instead of eggs. Children often wrote their names and addresses on the shell of an egg - accompanied by a message, and they invariably received a reply from a grateful recipient. Following the end of the Great War, the last collection was made on Thursday 27 March 1919 at which time, some 695,312 eggs had been collected by the girls of the townships of the district - and it was announced that Garstang Union had collected more eggs than any other district in the country. The township of Pilling was the most successful with 88,071 eggs collected. St. Michael's girls came third behind Knott End/Preesall. In the photograph are: Back row, left to right; Margaret Mary Rawcliffe, Margaret Horn, Elizabeth Whewell, Elizabeth Seed: front row seated on ground; Bertha Fox, Ethel Pickett.

Right: *ST. MICHAEL'S on WYRE. The Museum. photo c.1929:* St. Michael's Museum was founded by Hugh Phipps Hornby Esq., J.P. c.1894/5 in the 'old village school'. A small number of items are pictured outside the museum and include: (1) A Halberd which belonged to Thomas Robert Wilson-ffrance Esq., of Rawcliffe Hall. (2) A Push Plough. (19th century). (3) & (4) Flails for threshing corn, consisting simply of two strong sticks joined together by a strip of leather. (5) & (6) Crossbows (c.1800). (7) & (8) Salmon poaching implements (a spear and a cleek), captured from poachers on the River Lune. (9) (10) & (11) A number of querns (stone handmills) for grinding grain, found in a ditch at Staynall. (12) A stone '60 lb' weight - the weight of a bushel of wheat or a truss of new hay. (probably early 17th century). (13) A Belgian clog - thought to be the same pattern worn by Flemish weavers who came to Lancashire in the 14th century - from which the familiar Lancashire clog with leather uppers was fashioned. (14) & (15) Pre-historic perforated stone axe heads and an adze found at Pilling and Staynall. (16) A cast iron firegrate on castors from Mains Hall, previously owned by W.J.Fitzherbert-Brockholes Esq. The museum closed following the death of H.P.Hornby Esq., in 1944. Many exhibits were returned to their owners whilst others were taken to the Grundy House Museum in Blackpool. A large number of rare stuffed animals and birds were in poor condition, and were destroyed. A catalogue of exhibits may be seen in some local museums.

ALBERT CLAYTON'S

LARBRECK, c.1907: Photograph by R.W.Lord of Poulton. The previously thatched cottages, situated close to the roadside on the summit of Larbreck Hill, were a familiar landmark for over 200 years to travellers between Garstang and Poulton until the early 1960s. The last residents were Mrs George Dobson, who lived in the cottage nearest the camera. Mrs Dobson's daughter and son-in-law (Mr and Mrs Smith) and their family, lived in the second cottage. Some of the interior walls were made of clay and straw, and large oak beams supported the upstairs rooms. In 1962, the cottages were condemned; the families moved out in March 1963, and the cottages were demolished shortly afterwards; for many years, these were 'tied cottages' to nearby farms which were owned by Joseph Pyke & Co, provender merchants of Preston.

GREAT ECCLESTON, The Square, c.1900: Throughout the 19th century, the White Bull Hotel on the left of the photograph used to have its own bowling green. In 1887 Dr. R. H. Williams, the celebrated local doctor and J.P., described the great annual fair, which was held in The Square at the beginning of the reign of Queen Victoria, as the the time when 500 or 600 stallholders came to Great Eccleston from all over the country, arriving almost overnight, selling a wide and varied selection of goods. The fair attracted great crowds from all over the Fylde: at that time, almost every house in Great Eccleston sold goods of one sort or another.

West End. Eccleston.

GREAT ECCLESTON, The Smithy, c.1917: The right hand half of Critchley's Smithy was later converted into a small cottage known as Blazing Stump Cottage - the left hand half became Thomason's shoemaker's shop; the building still exists today. The last occupant of the cottage was Miss Martha Nicholson. In 1824 there was a barn on this site, and there was also a tithe barn down Butts Lane just beyond the smithy. Butts Lane also led to turf dales which were situated on what is now Great Eccleston Showfield. During the 18th and 19th centuries, the two small whitewashed cottages in the photograph, and a number of others in the village, obtained their fuel from turf dales.

GREAT ECCLESTON, The Bowling Green Hotel, c.1904: The landlord at the time was William Henry Newton. The licence was surrendered c.1907 and the premises then became known as Great Eccleston Tea Rooms. The 'Inn' was in existence at the beginning of the 19th century - owned at that time by Thomas Lawson, whilst the landlord was William Bennett. The premises were offered for sale on Wednesday 23 January 1839 and included a 'Brewhouse, Barn or Coach house, three Stables, a Shippon, outbuildings and two large gardens,' but at that time there was no mention of a bowling green. The bowling green was situated on the corner of Chesham Street and Leckonby Street, to the rear of the hotel. The premises are said to date from the beginning of the 18th century. In the 1920's the premises became a garage owned by John Hornby, and in 1928 the present owners, the Holden family took possession.

ELSWICK, Tower View, 1906:
The aftermath of the disastrous
fire at Tower View, otherwise
known as Cock Robin Row, in
Grange Lane, which occurred
on the evening of Monday 15
October 1906. The furniture of
all the occupants was safely
removed, and the only loss
suffered by the inhabitants was
by Jonathan Dobson in whose
house the fire started.
Jonathan lost a gold Albert
chain valued at £2. The
property was insured.

TREALES, Baling hay at Hesketh's, Cardwell's Farm, c.1916: During the Great War, the War Office formed Agricultural Battalions, consisting mainly of men who were considered to be ill suited for combat, to work on farms and supply produce such as hay for feeding the large numbers of horses in France and Belgium. At haytime, the members of these Battalions were often assisted by members of other Corps. George Davies, who lived at Stanley Farm St. Michael's and later at Carver's Bridge Cottage, Sowerby, is standing third from the left. It is likely that the Ruston baler belonged to Isaac Ball of Wharles.

TREALES, The Windmill, c.1890s: An outstanding photograph by B. Hargreaves of Poulton Street, Kirkham. During a gale on 27 January 1862, three of the sails of Treales Mill, which had only recently been refitted, were blown down and badly damaged: by the late 1920s the mill had become derelict, and it has since been converted into a private residence. On Monday 7 January 1839 and again on Sunday 26 September 1875, Carleton windmill ('Dick's Mill') was also severely damaged by high winds, having its cap and sails almost totally destroyed on each occasion.

KIRKHAM, Town End, c.1904: A fine view of Town End with men at work repairing the road with a steam roller. At this time there was no need for road signs or traffic cones, and there was no danger from passing motorists. The St. George Hotel is shown before its conical shaped 'tower' was removed.

ALBERT CLAYTON'S

WEETON, The Green, c.1907: Photograph by R.W.Lord of Poulton. The cottages in the photograph were known as Elmwood Cottages. In 1907, the thatched cottage in the centre of the picture was also a grocery shop occupied by Fanny Alice Ward. The cottages were demolished c.1964/5, and a bungalow now occupies the site. The lane on the right, which is known as Mill Lane by some local people - despite the local council re-naming it Kirkham Road, used to lead to Weeton windmill which was demolished c.1960.

WEETON, The Eagle & Child Hotel, c.1910: The 'Inn' is one of the Fylde's oldest licensed premises. It has held a licence since c.1585 (The licensing of ale houses began c.1552). The licensee in 1910 was James Valentine. In more recent times, in the early 1980s, a unit of the Irish Republican Army planned to explode a bomb inside the public house because it was frequented by soldiers who were stationed at the nearby Weeton Army Camp. The mounting steps for horse riders, and the column (inscribed 1755) which probably once supported a sun dial, are still in existence.

FORGOTTEN FYLDE ALBUM

SINGLETON, The Miller Arms Hotel, c.1909. **The hotel sign is of particular interest because it was painted by two well known Victorian artists - W.P.Frith of Derby Day fame, and Augustus Egg, who was famous for painting nudes. The sign was sought after for the Festival of Britain in 1951, and it was later sold at auction at Singleton Hall - the home of the Miller family who had been wealthy mill owners in Preston.**

INSKIP, The Reading Room, c.1904: **The reading room was formerly a thatched cottage and formed part of Lord Derby's estate. The cottage, shown in the photograph with a corrugated tin roof, was always known as the 'Old Reading Room' up to the time of its demolition c.1930s, although it had ceased to be a reading room c.1890s: it was situated mid way between Carr's Green Common and the Derby Arms Hotel, at the end of a short lane leading to Green Nook Farm: there is no record of when this cottage became the reading room, but it is likely that it was after 1848 when the Rev. Arthur Sharples became the first vicar of St. Peter's Church, Inskip. The last family to live here was Jim Myerscough and his wife Minnie (nee Bamber). During the latter half of the 19th century, local vicars encouraged the use of reading rooms, firstly to satisfy a quest for knowledge (newspapers were usually available), and secondly to provide leisure activities in an attempt to keep young men out of the public houses, and to prevent them drifting into the towns to seek higher paid employment.**

Above: *INSKIP, The Mill, c.1934:* In the early part of this century,
Bamber and Rowe, Cheese Factors in Orchard Street, Preston, went
round the farms in the Fylde, buying up good quality cheese. In 1932,
Tom Rowe started to make his own cheese at Inskip Mill (which he
called the Model Dairy), to sell in his shop in Preston. The first
cheese maids he employed were Mary Bamber from Woodplumpton,
and Elizabeth Shorrock from Stanley Farm, Roseacre. Production
commenced using about a dozen of Gornall's 50 gallon cheese tubs.
As business improved, Tom Rowe employed more staff - some girls
had to cycle 7 or 8 miles to work every morning, and were paid 30
shillings for a 7 day working week - often working from 7 a.m. to 9
p.m. The girls received a 2/6d wage increase when a shift system was
introduced. Tom owned his own wagons, and the drivers brought in
milk in 10 gallon kits from villages all over the Fylde. Local farmers
brought in their own milk, and received a slightly higher price for it.
The factory produced mainly Lancashire cheese although towards
the end of the 1930s, whey-butter and Cheddar cheese were
introduced. At Christmas time, sage cheese was also produced. Tom
Rowe, seen with his back to the camera, lived at York House,
Bilsborrow and died on 22 October 1956. The old mill was
demolished in late 1991 and early 1992, at which time, massive
blocks of sandstone were excavated; these had originally supported
the steam engine which had powered the mill. New houses have
since been built on the site.

Right: *INSKIP, The Temperance Inn, c.1924:* The inn was formerly
known as The Old Hall Inn. During the 19th century, most of the
houses and inhabitants of the village of Inskip were located within
400 yards of this site. The 20th century has seen a shift in population
as new houses have been built near the church. The licence of the
old inn was surrendered by Lord Shuttleworth on 13 February 1904 at
Garstang Licensing Sessions, at which time he expressed his desire
that the Justices would not grant a licence within one mile of these
premises, which then became a Temperance Inn. Inskip formerly had
a public house known as the Cavendish Arms, owned by the
Cavendish family of Holker Hall until around the mid 1850s - it was
situated 200 yards from the present Derby Arms Hotel whilst
travelling north towards Inskip Church.

SOWERBY, Swan Cottages, 1904: **The Parish Registers of St. Michael's on Wyre list a number of members of the Swan family living at 'Sowrbie' in the 17th century. In 1676 for instance, 'Ellizabeth (sic) daughter to Jonathan Swanne of Sowrbie' was christened on 24 September. It is likely that the Swan family lived here at that time. The cottages, which were demolished in 1940, were situated near the council houses in Sowerby, close to the site of the present telephone box.**

CATFORTH, The Sports Club, 1924: **The Sports Club was built in late 1922, early 1923, as a War Memorial to the men of Catforth who fell in the Great War. Catforth Village Hall was built at the same time and was considered to be the 'official' War Memorial. The Sports Club cost around £1200 to build and was officially opened on 1 February 1923 by W.J.Walmsley, Esq., of Bartle Hall; its facilities included a billiard table, a first class maple dance floor, tennis courts, and a football field. The Club fell into decline at the beginning of World War II and was sold by the trustees to Mr. Jim Ball, a garage proprietor; it remains in use as a garage today (1995).**

CATFORTH, The Village, c.1905: Photograph by Frederick Cooper of Preston. The Bay Horse Beerhouse is situated on the left of the photograph - the landlord at this time was William Jenkinson. The shop on the right of the picture was rebuilt in 1913 and is now the Post Office. The Post Office in 1905 was situated in a cottage down the lane beyond the 'Bay Horse' - the Postmaster at that time was Thomas Hesketh.

BARTLE, Lea & Salwick Brass Band, c.1907: Lea and Salwick Brass Band is seen outside the house known as Barnfield - owned at the time by John Cartmell. Many Fylde villages had their own band during the 19th century, but very few are now in existence. The front of the house is seen as it was originally built in 1834 - the bay windows and the doorway have since been altered on two occasions. The Band played at Woodplumpton and Catforth Schools field day. The children had walked in procession from Catforth school on their way to Bartle Hall, the home of Major Charles Birley, where they played games and were regaled with tea, cakes and fruit. A halt was made at Barnfield in order to give the children a rest. The house was later to be owned by Mr. T.C.Rainford, the well known Preston butcher. Barnfield is now a Nursing Home, having been considerably extended in recent years.

WOODPLUMPTON, The Old Post Office, c.1924: The proprietor at this time was Joseph Parker. The Post Office and shop was later purchased in 1926 by John Joseph Whalley and his wife Mary whose daughter Elizabeth had previously worked for Joseph Parker from the age of 13 years. Elizabeth ran the business whilst her father went out to work at Winnard's Corn Mill in Woodplumpton. Mr. Whalley's first days takings were 16 shillings - the Post Office paid him £3.12 shillings per month. Elizabeth married Jack Pickup in September 1933 and they stayed here until the 1960s when they moved to Danson Hill Farm at Eaves. In 1926 the Post Office did not have an electricity supply, and water was obtained from a pump in the back kitchen which was connected to an underground well. The water supply frequently ran dry, and by 1959 the building in the photograph was considered to be unsuitable for use as a shop, and it was demolished; it was replaced by the present Post Office in the same year.

WOODPLUMPTON, The Old Workhouse. c.1905: The Corn Mill (formerly the Workhouse) was owned at this time by John Rigby who was also a coal merchant, operating from the adjoining canal wharf. John Kendall had been a previous tenant of the mill. The workhouse was built in 1823 at a cost of £1200 including 2 acres of land; it was built to house up to 72 inmates, but records show that in the year 1841 there were 83 inhabitants. The workhouse closed c.1864; it was replaced by Preston Union Workhouse which was built at Fulwood in 1868.

46

SALWICK, John Knowles's Wheelwright and Joiner's Shop, c.1908: The joiner's Shop was situated next door to William Parker's Smithy. At the rear of the premises there was a saw-pit, and one of the original saws used in the saw-pit remains in the possession of the Parker family. Pictured left to right:- James T. Parker (born 1889); Arthur Eccles; Jim Fletcher; D. Robinson; Edmund Hindle; John Knowles; William Parker. The old smithy is still in existence, and is now a petrol filling station.

SECTION 5

West of Garstang & Over Wyre

NATEBY HALL, c.1890s: Photograph by H. Jackson of Cleckheaton. It is likely that there has been a house on or near this site since the 13th century when the Travers family settled here - where they remained until the early 17th century. In 1818, the estate formed part of the Kirkland Hall estate of Thomas Butler Cole, Esq. In the Spring of 1853, Nateby Hall estate was let with vacant possession at which time it was described as being 257 acres 2 roods and 37 perches (Statute measure) in extent. Nateby Hall estate was bought in 1868 by Col. John Wilson-Patten (who was later to become Lord Winmarleigh), from William Bashall Esq., of Farington Lodge. The old house burnt down in 1870/1 and the house in the photograph was built, but this presented little to show of former splendour. Lord Winmarleigh died in 1892, and his estate passed to his eldest son's widow who re-married, and leased the estate for shooting to Messrs. Fletcher and Waters, two American millionaires. After her death in 1912, a large part of the estate was bought by Mr. Frank Reddaway, a wealthy Manchester rubber manufacturer, but Nateby Hall itself (240 acres) was sold for £7000 to James Martland of Burscough. The house gradually fell into a state of decay, and it was demolished in October 1969. At the time of its demolition, an unsuccessful search was made for a legendary tunnel linking it with Bowers House at Nateby. A new house has since been built on the site.

NATEBY, Caton's Farm, c.1906: Dorothy Jackson, daughter of Isaac Jackson who farmed here, is seen outside her home; she married Fred Parker from London, who went to work at Nateby during World War I. The late James Jackson (Dorothy's brother), told me that the farm had been extended on a number of occasions as more land was brought into cultivation from the wild moss. When a farmer became a little more prosperous, a larger house was required to accommodate not only an increasing family, but also extra workmen who lived in. The farm formed part of the estate of William Bashall Esq., of Farington who purchased the Nateby estate in 1853 from the trustees of the late Duke of Hamilton. The Nateby estate was bought for £45,700, and included Pilling Moor, Tarnacre and Nateby - a total of 1,802 acres. When Mr. Bashall died, the estate was divided between his two sons - William taking property in Nateby and John inheriting the Bowerswood estate and land in Bonds. On the death of William, the Nateby estate passed to his daughter who had married Mr. Norris Bretherton of Leyland. Mr and Mrs Bretherton then went to live at Bowerswood House, Nateby.

Above: *NATEBY, The Cat House Inn, c.1870s:* The Cat House Inn was licensed as a beerhouse. Mary Bamber was the landlady from c.1850 until c.1885 and she also owned a small farm - the sign over the doorway reads, 'Mary Bamber, Licensed Retailer of Ale & Porter.' The premises in the photograph were demolished before 1900 and a new inn was built. The inn continued as a beerhouse until c.1928 when the nearby XL Hotel was built, at which time the licence was transferred to the new hotel. The Bamber, and later the Chippendale families (related by marriage), owned the old Cat House Inn until it was demolished in 1989.

Right: *OUT RAWCLIFFE, Haytime at Hudson's Farm, c.1921:* A nostalgic scene during haytime at Out Rawcliffe - bringing in the hay was known as 'housing'. Jim Swarbrick of Hudson's Farm is on the haystack on the left, and his brother Bill is on the cart with Jim's son (also called Jim). Bill Swarbrick lived at Dockinsall Farm, Dry Bread Lane, Out Rawcliffe and worked as a blacksmith for Jonathan Collinson of Longmoor Lane, Nateby. In the 19th century, hay was weighed as follows: a truss of old hay weighed 56 lbs, whilst a truss of new hay weighed 60 lbs - 36 trusses comprised a load, and hay became old on the 1st of September.

OUT RAWCLIFFE, The Old Cobbler's Shop, Moss Edge, 1899: **Henry Swarbrick and his family, pictured in the doorway of his cobbler's shop - pictured left to right are: Henry Swarbrick, William Jackson Swarbrick (born 18 Feb 1893), James Gradwell Swarbrick (born 28 Jan 1891), and Jane Swarbrick. The shop was moved to Hudson's Cottage in Out Rawcliffe c.1920s when James Gradwell Swarbrick became the local cobbler. The old building exists today at Willow Farm, Out Rawcliffe.**

THRESHING DAY IN THE FYLDE, c.1905: **A photograph taken by Edward Brook of 3 Preston Road, Marton. It is a scene which was enacted at most farms in the Fylde well into the 1940's.**

ALBERT CLAYTON'S

OUT RAWCLIFFE, The Farmers' Club on board the P.S. Lady Moyra, 3 August 1910: The Paddle Steamer was named after Lady Moyra Cavendish of Holker Hall (P.S. *Lady Margaret* and P.S. *Lady Evelyn* were two sister ships). Lady Evelyn Cavendish later became the Duchess of Devonshire and moved to Chatsworth House. Out Rawcliffe Farmers' Club was formed in 1853 by Thomas Robert Wilson-ffrance Esq., of Rawcliffe Hall, Jocelyn C. Westby, Esq., and the Rev. William Hornby, Vicar of St. Michael's. The principal aims of the Club were to encourage competition in agricultural products; ploughing, and to improve the bloodstock of cattle and other farm animals. The first event to take place in connection with the Club was a ploughing match on land near Rawcliffe Hall on Tuesday 1 March 1853 when over 20 competitors took part. The double plough prize was awarded to William Sherdley, whilst the single plough prize winner was Thomas Cross. After the presentation of prizes, a dinner was held at the Cartford Inn. T.R. Wilson-ffrance did not live to see the Club prosper - he died on 7 October 1853. Although the Club was formed in 1853, Rawcliffe ploughing matches had been held prior to 1840. Among those in the photograph are Thomas Lund (landlord of the Cartford Inn), T. C. Southward, of Crookgate Farm (both seated on left) - Joe Tunstall (3rd from right), and Tom Winchester, the schoolmaster, on the extreme left.

STALMINE, c.1922/3: A splendid farming scene in the Fylde showing Harry Steele with a pair of Shire horses at Cardwell's, Well House Farm, Stalmine, where he worked as head teamsman. In 1924, he married Jenny Pye of Hankinson's Farm, Stalmine - he died in 1969 aged 69 years. Harry is seen wearing fustian trousers, clogs and leggings, all typical wearing apparel for a farm worker.

HAMBLETON, The Shard Bridge Hotel, c.1907: Photograph by R.W.Lord of Poulton. The bridge was built in 1864 at a cost of £13,800. In March 1906 an attempt was made to free Shard bridge and to buy out its shareholders for £9500, thus freeing the bridge of its tolls. A number of meetings were held in local parishes where it was hoped to raise £2000, and Mr. Robert Winder of Rawcliffe Lodge promised £200. However, hopes were finally dashed when Sir W. Hulton, Chairman of Lancashire County Council Main Bridges Sub-Committee announced that unless the whole of the money could be raised locally to buy out the shareholders, there was no prospect of freeing the bridge as the L.C.C. had withdrawn their support. It was to be a further 87 years (18 July 1993) before a new toll free bridge was opened and the old Shard bridge was demolished. It was to this hotel that the eccentric young squire of Out Rawcliffe - Robert John Barton Wilson-ffrance, sought assistance, on Sunday 22 August 1875: he arrived at the toll gate at 2 a.m. with his horse and carriage, on the Poulton side of the bridge, just as the tide was coming in, to find that the gatekeeper was in bed. The squire foolishly attempted to ford the river in the darkness, accompanied by a female companion, but when the conveyance reached mid stream, the force of the incoming tide swept the horse and carriage upstream, upsetting the occupants into the river. After some difficulty, the squire rescued the terrified young woman, and they went to the Shard Bridge Hotel to seek assistance. Unfortunately for him, the landlord had heard of his wild escapades and would not assist him. The horse was rescued at 5a.m, deeply embedded in mud on the bank of the River Wyre.

STALMINE, The Seven Stars Hotel, c.1905: A fine view outside this well known watering place, with a wagonette from Blackpool en-route for Knott End, on what was known as the green route by cab proprietors. Amongst the trees in the background stands St. James's Church where the Rev. Joseph Rowley was incumbent - albeit in his absence - for 64 years; he was prison chaplain at Lancaster Castle for 54 years until his resignation in 1858, in his 85th year. As prison chaplain at Lancaster Castle he attended to the spiritual needs of 170 unfortunate prisoners whilst they prepared themselves for death by public hanging. It is said that during the 54 years of his chaplaincy, he had never been absent from his duties for more than two consecutive Sundays. The Rev. Joseph Rowley died on 3 January 1864.

ALBERT CLAYTON'S

STALMINE, The Seven Stars Hotel and the Pack Horse Inn, c.1906: The Pack Horse Inn has been converted into a grocery store and a Post Office; the present postmistress being the great grand-daughter of Jane Porter, who was Postmistress in the Post Office attached to the Seven Stars Hotel (on the left of the photograph). The original mahogany bar from the Pack Horse Inn has been retained, and is now used as the Post Office counter; the floor tiles which date back to the 19th century, have been also preserved. A telegraph service opened at Stalmine and Pilling Post Offices on Tuesday 21 February 1894.

STALMINE with STAYNALL, Ye Wardleys Toffee Shop, c.1905: Ann Swarbrick married Robert Hornby, and started to make a sweetmeat called Wardleys Mint Cake around 1861. Ann later produced Wardleys Toffee which came in two varieties - butter toffee and treacle toffee. Ann's father was William Swarbrick (born 1816), a well known ferryman who saved a number of lives, and worked the River Wyre, musselling and fishing for over 50 years. Ann continued to make toffee well into the 20th century; she died in 1932 aged 92 years. The photograph shows Ann selling toffee to a young lad at the door of her windswept home. The house is situated overlooking the River Wyre, approximately 100 yards on the Hambleton side of the Wardleys Hotel, and has since been extensively modernised. Note the bricks and grass on the roof ; and the water butt - which was used to collect water for washing.

PILLING, Lady's Hill, c.1906:
Lady's Hill is described in the Tithe Maps and in the 1871 Parish Magazine as Lazy Hill, where there used to be an inn near the shore, and there was another inn at the other end of the village - both of which had bowling greens, and were in existence in 1712-14 - they were called The Providence, and The Black Bull. Lady's Hill is situated near the Golden Ball Hotel (built 1904). The 1871 Parish Magazine describes how, in former times, one of the inns was situated in what was known as Higher End Lane - to distinguish it from Pilling Lane, now in the township of Preesall, which was then designated Lower End Lane. In the late 19th century, Pilling caused great concern to the Garstang Board of Guardians. The Medical Officer, Dr. Thomas Fisher, and the nuisance officer, reported that most of the houses in Pilling were unfit for habitation - drinking water

was unfit for consumption, and toilet facilities were extremely primitive. The incidence of water borne diseases was higher in Pilling than in any other township in Garstang Union. The surrounding roads were also in poor condition - it had long been the custom for farmers to repair their own stretch of road using sand or stones taken from the shore.

PILLING, c.1920's: The location is unknown but there is no doubt about the ownership of the horse and cart. William and Ellen Redman lived in Bradshaw Lane, Pilling. The cart is shown laden with live hens and 112 lbs bags of potatoes - all to be carried by two of their daughters, Edith and Ada.

Opposite, Centre: *PREESALL, Mill Lane, c.1905:* A fine animated view of Mill Lane, so named because Preesall's old wooden peg mill was situated at the top of the hill before it was completely demolished during the worst storm of the 19th century, which occurred in the early hours of Monday 7 January 1839: there had been a peg mill on Preesall Hill since at least the year 1690. A new brick tower mill was built near the side of the road to Stalmine in 1839 - the mill house was built in 1846. According to Moore's Almanac of 1815, windmills were 'invented' in the year 1299 - it is not known when they first appeared in the Fylde, although it is said that there were two mills at Lytham over a century earlier in 1191: these early mills were wooden peg or post mills. As corn production increased towards the end of the 18th century, the more familiar and substantial brick tower mills were built. In 1929, the owner of Preesall Hill, Mr. W. Heald of Village Farm, offered the hill for sale to the local council. It is said to contain large amounts of the finest sand which is suitable for making artificial stone, but the council considered that he was asking too much for it, and they decided against buying it.

Opposite, Bottom: *PREESALL, Railway Station and Bridge, c.1907:* A rare period photograph showing construction underway of Fordstone road bridge, and Preesall railway station. The material for the embankment is being excavated from the area to the right of the bridge; the excavated section later became a lake. It can be seen that the foundations of the station buildings are already in place, and a temporary platform had been built. Note the small white area under the bridge - this was part of the old road which was abandoned when the new road over the bridge was opened. A short length of the original road can still be seen leading to Preesall Bowling Club. The single line railway was extended from Pilling to Knott End - being officially opened on Thursday 30 July 1908 - thus completing the Garstang to Knott End railway. The initial length of line from Garstang to Pilling was opened on 5 December 1870. The contractor for the Garstang to Pilling section was a Mr. Bush, whose brother-in-law John Rothwell, who also worked on the line, was killed by a train at Garstang and Catterall station in May 1872.

PREESALL, Saturday 30 June 1906: Councillor R. Cardwell of Preesall U.D.C. was presented with a silver key after inaugurating Preesall's new water supply. The ceremony was witnessed by many local civic dignitaries. To demonstrate the water power, the party went to the top of Preesall Hill where a jet of water approximately 50 feet high was projected over the school, itself some 133 feet above sea level. Out of 335 local houses only 164 initially took the water supply, but as soon as the others realised the great benefits to be gained in having 'water on tap', they began to apply to have their homes connected. Following the opening ceremony, the officials had dinner at the Saracen's Head Inn, and afterwards they went on a drive in wagonettes round Cockerham and Winmarleigh. The estimated cost of providing Preesall's water supply in 1905 was £13,750. A total of 30 miles of mains, and 16 miles of local service pipes had been laid during the winter months of 1905/6.

PREESALL, Town Foot, c.1904: In April and May 1876, specialist borers from Middlesborough were seen to be drilling (for iron ore) near Town Foot at Preesall, and rumours quickly spread that a great deposit of salt had been found deep beneath the ground. The findings were kept secret at the time, but the rumours proved to be correct. The original business was run by Fleetwood Salt Co. but they were taken over in 1890 by the United Alkali Co. Boreholes were sunk, and brine was pumped across the River Wyre to Burn Naze refinery where it was converted into salt. On Monday 24 March 1890, the first consignment of salt to be produced at Burn Naze refinery (about 250 tons), was shipped to Bristol from Wyre Dock at Fleetwood. Shafts were eventually sunk at Preesall (c.1893), and an enormous cavern was excavated some 450 feet feet below ground, where blocks of salt were cut and brought to the surface. Large pillars about 60 feet square were left in place to support the roof.

The workers, some of whom had come from the extensive salt mines at Nantwich in Cheshire, worked by candlelight as there was no danger from methane gas. On 9th and 10th of August 1923, and also later in the month, the mine flooded and the pillars of salt melted. The ground shook violently, subsiding around 150 feet, and large depressions were formed. Farm roads, a farm, and ten fine beech trees vanished into the abyss. Loud rumblings were heard coming from deep beneath the surface of the ground. The area became the venue for hundreds of interested sightseers who arrived in charabancs: these lakes are still visible today near Town Foot.

KNOTT END, The Railway Station, c.1909: The Manning Wardle 0-6-0 side tank engine *Knott End* about to leave Knott End station for Garstang with four newly acquired bogie saloons, and a four wheeled brake passenger coach, shortly after the line was extended to Knott End. The extension of the line proved to be a boon to the Preesall Salt Company who, in 1913, transported almost 8,000 tons of salt. The railway was also used for transporting agricultural produce, coal, and large quantities of peat from the extensive peat reserves at Pilling (the industry provided employment for large numbers of local men). On Wednesday 15 May 1895, a goods train carrying peat moss litter, arrived at Nateby station with two of its trucks on fire. The sparks from the engine had ignited the dry peat - the fire was fanned by the breeze, and the trucks were left to their fate. A wire spark arrester was then fitted to the funnel of the engine. The Knott End Railway Company is said to have been the first railway company in the country to use corridor passenger coaches.

ALBERT CLAYTON'S

KNOTT END, Lancaster Road, c.1910: A leisurely scene in Knott End with a fruit and vegetable salesman blocking the road with his cart. Beyond the fruit cart can be seen the gable end of Dolly's Cottage - probably Knott End's most photographed landmark. In February 1935 it was decided that Dolly's Cottage had to be demolished because its exposed position in the road presented a hazard to traffic; this caused great distress to the two elderly ladies who lived there, both of whom were reluctant to leave, having lived there for many years. Miss Emsley, one of the residents, had provided an annual tea party for the local children in the Methodist School - she left Knott End to live with relatives in Manchester. Miss Jane Shepherd, the other resident, suffered ill health as a result of being forced to move from her home. When the house was finally demolished, it was discovered that the upstairs 'walls' were made of sailcloth which had been whitewashed for generations. The roof was originally thatched, but it was later covered in corrugated tin sheets. A lintel inscribed with the date 1732, was above the door in the left hand porch. The lintel has since been built into the sea wall at Knott End, and can be seen today.

KNOTT END, The Post Office, c.1905: By 1909, the Post Office had been moved to a new location on the opposite side of the road, in a shop next to the Methodist Church. The 1851 census returns show that the population of Knott End was 118, including a grocer, a publican, an unemployed shoemaker, a tide-watcher, and a number of fishermen. On Friday 19 June 1818, a group of farmers, and other young men from the Fylde, arranged a fishing trip in two boats off Knott End. However, they met with little success so they decided to have a race. The crew of the slower of the two boats hoisted extra sail in order to increase speed, but a sudden squall of wind overturned the craft in a deep part of the River Wyre, and the boat sank almost at once. The six occupants were drowned before their companions could manoeuvre their boat into a position where the unfortunate men could be rescued: they were John Dickinson, John Ronson and John Lord of Pilling; William Croft of Preesall, John Bradley of Nateby, and William Longworth, a farrier from Garstang. As the tide ebbed, a search was made for the bodies, and two of them (Ronson and Croft) were recovered.

SECTION 6

Poulton, Fleetwood & Blackpool

POULTON le FYLDE, Saturday 13 February, 1904: In the Spring of 1903, the sitting member for the Blackpool Division, Mr. H.W.Worsley-Taylor, M.P. announced that he intended to resign from Parliament: he had been criticised for his poor attendance, and for not making his maiden speech. At a meeting held in Preston, the Tories appointed a successor: Wilfred W. Ashley, Esq., who was a member of the Shaftesbury family - a son of a former member of Gladstone's Cabinet, and son-in-law of multi-millionaire Sir Edward Cassell. Ashley visited all parts of the constituency, making rousing speeches in anticipation of a forthcoming by-election; he went to live at 'The Knowle' in Blackpool, and established himself as a most popular figure. King Edward VII was godfather to his daughter; he was on friendly terms with the Duke and Duchess of Devonshire, and the Duke and Duchess of Connaught; all of whom were frequent visitors to his home. Ashley was knowledgeable on national and local issues, and his Liberal opponent Mr. Vivian Phillips, acknowledged the difficulty in fighting an election against him, describing him as "one of the best fellows in the world." However, Worsley-Taylor refused to resign, and Ashley had to wait until the election of January 1906, when he defeated his Liberal opponent (Phillips) by 3061 votes. In the photograph, Ashley is seen in Poulton Market Place driving a new car which had been loaned to him to carry out his 'electioneering' - almost two years before the election took place. The registration number of the car was AA 35 - a Hampshire County Council allocation.

POULTON le FYLDE, Bull Street, 1904: The landlord of 'The Bull Hotel' in 1904 was Joseph Bleasdale. The Bull Hotel is thought to be one of the oldest public houses in Poulton - dating back to the 16th century. In the 1890s, whilst alterations were being carried out, a number of coins dating back to the reign of Queen Elizabeth I, and a peculiar wooden whistle about 8 inches long, identified as being Elizabethan in character, were found. The old cellars used to be vaulted in a similar manner to the vaults in ancient Abbeys. The premises shown in the photograph were pulled down c.1959/60 and a new hotel was built - no trace remains of the ancient structure.

POULTON le FYLDE, Dudley Hall, c.1892: Photograph by H. Jackson of Cleckheaton. Dudley Hall was situated on Bull Street - it was one of Poulton's last thatched houses, and may be seen in the distance in the photograph which features the Bull Hotel.

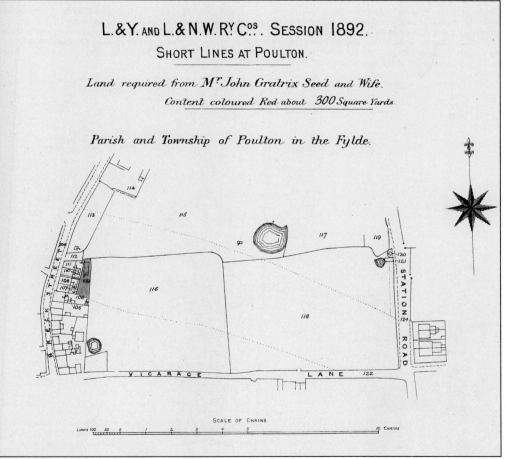

L.&Y. AND L.&N.W. RY. Cᵒˢ. SESSION 1892.

SHORT LINES AT POULTON.

Land required from Mʳ John Gratrix Seed and Wife.
Content coloured Red about 300 Square Yards.

Parish and Township of Poulton in the Fylde.

POULTON le FYLDE, 22 April 1893: Plan of a plot of land measuring 300 square yards (No. 109 on the plan) belonging to John Gratrix Seed and Mary, his wife. The land was to be compulsorily purchased under the authority of The Lancashire & Yorkshire Railway (Various Powers) Act, 1892, as part of the overall scheme to replace the original Poulton station, in order to eliminate the dangerous curve in the line near the site of the 'old' station, which was situated at the junction of Station Road and Breck Road. John Gratrix Seed and Mary also owned an adjoining plot of land which included a 'Dwellinghouse, garden, green house, yard, outbuildings and passage in common,' numbered 106 on the plan (also measuring 300 square yards), in the occupation of Mr. Robert Parkinson. On Wednesday 25 March 1896, Colonel Addison, the Board of Trade Inspector, officially examined the new section of line and gave permission for the opening of the line to traffic. The contractors were Messrs. E. Taylor & Sons of Littleborough.

Right: *POULTON le FYLDE, The Old Railway Station, c.1890s:* The station, which was built c.1840 when the Preston/Wyre railway was built, was situated near the junction of Breck Road and Station Road. Prior to 1846, passengers travelling to Blackpool had to travel by road from Poulton, but in April of that year, the line was extended from Poulton to Blackpool. At this time, a dangerous curve was built in the line immediately beyond Poulton station, and a speed limit of 6 m.p.h. was introduced. However, despite a number of accidents (some fatal), drivers continued to exceed the speed limit. In May 1893, a Poulton solicitor, Mr. H. Parry, wrote to the joint owners of the line (The London North Western Railway, and The Lancashire & Yorkshire Railway) warning them of the dire consequences they would face if an accident was to occur on this dangerous, almost semi-circular curve, as a result of excessive speed. With the increase in holiday traffic, it was recognised that there was a serious problem

on this stretch of line, and on Saturday 1 July 1893, the railway companies completed the purchase of a large plot of land on which to build another station, on a new site, which would eliminate the danger. However, at 11 p.m. on that same evening, an excursion train left Blackpool for Stockport - the driver, Cornelius Ridgway from Stockport, being unfamiliar with the line and uncertain of his location, approached the curve at between 50 and 60 m.p.h. The train left the rails, the engine ploughed on its side into an embankment, the tender overturned and the carriages were badly damaged. Three people (including the driver) were killed and over 30 were injured who were taken to the nearby Railway & Station Hotel, where the railway companies provided medical assistance, and unlimited refreshments for the rescuers. On Saturday 17 March 1894, Mrs Marsh, one of the injured passengers, brought an action against the railway companies at Liverpool Assizes. An offer of £1500 was accepted by Mrs Marsh for her own injuries, for the death of her husband, and on behalf of her 5 children. The railway station (pictured) was replaced by the present station in March 1896.

POULTON le FYLDE, The Wesleyan Chapel, c.1904: The chapel was situated on the corner of Chapel Street, the front of which looked out on to Queen's Square. Note the narrow cobbled street on the right of the photograph which was originally called Back Street - the name was later changed to Chapel Street - and also the Notice for the election of Councillors - Poulton became an Urban District in 1900. The original chapel was built c.1819, but it was replaced in 1861 by more commodious premises. In 1892, the chapel built in 1861 was 'razed to the ground' and replaced by the chapel shown in the photograph, being completely re-built in only 17 weeks at a cost of £1300; it was later extended and refurbished in 1907/8. The last service took place in December 1964.

FLEETWOOD, The P.S.Lady Moyra c.1910: Photograph by Edward Sankey of Barrow. The Furness Railway Company operated paddle steamers between Fleetwood and Barrow, carrying thousands of summer visitors to enjoy the beauty of the Lake District. Between 1st June and 12th August 1906, some 71,000 passengers had travelled on the P.S.*Lady Moyra*'s sister ships - the P.S.*Lady Evelyn* and the P.S.*Lady Margaret* (see photograph of Out Rawcliffe Farmers' Club on board P.S.*Lady Moyra* in August 1910). The P.S.*Lady Moyra* was built at Clydebank in 1905 - originally named *Gwalia* - she was bought by the Furness Railway Company in 1910 - and was requisitioned as a mine-sweeper in September 1914 during World War I. The P.S.*Lady Moyra* was sunk in 1940 at Dunkirk during World War II.

FLEETWOOD & KNOTT END MOTORS, c.1914: 'Andy' Parkinson's removal lorry at Knott End. The man standing second from the left is a Mr. Shaw. Knott End foreshore is visible in the background. Andy Parkinson's depot at Knott End was situated across the road from the Bourne Arms Hotel - he owned another depot in Fleetwood. The registration number of the lorry was B 5855.

BLACKPOOL, 1907: Photograph taken from the promenade near the Gynn on 25 June 1907. Four young people from Stourbridge visited Blackpool in June 1907; they stayed in a flat at the Gynn. On the morning of Tuesday 25th, the party went out onto the promenade to take some photographs. Dolly Gillam (24), a keen amateur photographer, set up her camera near the steps which led down to the sands. Whilst focussing her camera, a large wave swept her into the sea. Two of her companions - her brother and Ernest Taylor (her boyfriend - a non swimmer), jumped in after her. A lifebuoy was thrown in, but it failed to reach the helpless victims, who were dashed against the sea wall by the waves. One by one the victims disappeared under the water and were drowned. As the tide receded, all three bodies were found within 150 yards of each other. A large crowd gathered to watch the grim spectacle, and the photograph shows the scene as the bodies were being recovered. An inquest was held that evening and the jury returned a verdict of "Accidentally drowned".

JULIAN'S FAREWELL STUNT *BIDDING GOOD-BYE-EE TO THE MAYOR*

BLACKPOOL, TANK WEEK, Tuesday 26 February 1918: **Photograph by R.W.Lord. The fund raising tank *Julian,* had raised over £33,000,000 for the war effort (World War I), before it arrived in Blackpool for the start of Tank Week, (commencing Monday 18 February). During its stay near the fountain in Talbot Square in Blackpool, over £1,000,000 was raised - the Mayor, Councillor A. Lindsay Parkinson, J.P. donated £100,000 on behalf of the Council. In the photograph, the Mayor and other civic dignitaries are seen bidding farewell to the tank and its crew, who, as a parting gesture, surmounted two sandbagged entrenchments before leaving for Talbot Road railway station: his Worship had previously presented a silver cigarette case to each member of the crew. The Officer in charge, Lieut. H. Davies, complimented the Mayor, saying that in no other town had the Mayor shown such enthusiasm for the fund raising effort. Schoolchildren were given a holiday and hundreds lined the route to the station, cheering wildly as the tank passed by.**

BLACKPOOL, R.H.O.Hill's delivery van, c.1908: **R.H.O Hill's was one of Blackpool's best known stores - operating at this time from their 'bazaars' selling fancy goods and toys at 59, 60 & 68 Bank Hey Street, on what had been the site of a school which had been built in the early 19th century. On Wednesday 13 January 1932 and again during the early hours of Sunday 7 May 1967 their building was destroyed by fire. The premises were re-built and re-opened by R.H.O Hill's, but were later occupied by Messrs. Binns & Co. The building has recently been made into individual shop units, although at the present time, the premises are closed.**

ALBERT CLAYTON'S

BLACKPOOL, R.H.O.Hill's Store on fire: At 11 a.m. on Wednesday 13 January 1932, a serious fire broke out on the fourth floor in the 'Fairy Grotto' of R.H.O. Hill's bazaar. The fire spread quickly and within an hour the store lay in ruins, despite the combined efforts of Blackpool, St. Anne's and Blackpool Tower Co. fire brigades. Over 250 employees temporarily lost their jobs until the store was re-built.

BLACKPOOL, The Windmill Hotel, Layton, c.1907: Photograph by R.W.Lord of Poulton. The hotel was demolished c. 1975/6 and a modern public house has been built near the original site. In 1907, the licensee was Eliza King. The inn was formerly known as the Mill Inn. The cottages in the distance were demolished c.1923 when the road was widened. Hoo Hill windmill was situated across the road from the inn - on 17 July 1852, the windmill was hit by lightning and one of its sails was wrecked; the miller had just finished unwrapping the sailcloth when the lightning struck; the interior of the mill was also badly damaged, and the miller was fortunate to escape with his life. Lightning struck Hoo Hill windmill again during a severe storm in July 1881; the mill was severely damaged and was demolished c.1890s.

STAINING, The Windmill, c.1904: Photograph by J. Wolstenholme, 14 Peter Street, Blackpool. In December 1895 the sails of the mill were destroyed in a storm, and new sails made from oak and pitch pine were fitted in January 1896. The mill was one of the few tower mills in the Fylde to have canvas covered sails, and the cap had to be turned manually into the wind by the use of a rope. The structure was about 50 feet high with each sail measuring slightly over 30 feet: there were 4 pairs of millstones - the upper ones weighing about 2 tons each, and the lower ones about one and a half tons each. The mill had 3 floors, and the driving wheel measured 12 feet. It was owned by Mr. William Riding of Carleton and was occupied by Mr. Crampton, whose father had been miller here for 19 years. The mill, which is estimated to be over 200 years old, has been made into a house, and new 'sails' were fitted on Saturday 9 September 1989; these sails were destroyed during a gale after only a few months, but they have since been replaced.

BLACKPOOL, Gypsy Sarah Boswell and family on the sandhills at South Shore c.1885: Gypsy Sarah, the most famous of all Blackpool Gypsies, was born in Kent on 22 March 1805. Sarah went to Blackpool in 1827 where she lived at the northern end of the town, but went to live as a nomad on the sandhills at South Shore in 1836: she was born Sarah Hearn, and married Edward Boswell, thus uniting two well known Gypsy families. Edward (Ned), who was a cutler, died in 1892 aged 92 years. Sarah had grandparents who lived to be over 100 years of age: one is buried in Brindle Churchyard and the other is buried in Wales. The first time she saw a doctor was in August 1903 when he diagnosed old age! Sarah smoked a pipe all her life - right up to the time of her death - which occurred on Wednesday 2 March 1904, twenty days short of her 99th birthday. Sarah was laid in state in her tent on the sandhills, surrounded by her family; she had 9 children (4 were living at the time of her death), and she also left grandchildren, great grandchildren, and great, great, grandchildren to the 5th generation. Gypsy Sarah was a great believer in Gypsy customs, one of which was to burn the possessions of the dead, but her family preserved her belongings, including the old tramcar body in which she had told the fortunes of countless thousands of summer visitors to the resort: she passed on her 'magical' powers to her nieces. Gypsy Sarah had foretold of the postponement of the Coronation of King Edward VII, and predicted a Great War between Britain and foreign powers, which would not take place for 10 years after her death. A large crowd assembled in Layton Cemetery, where she was buried on Saturday 5 March 1904.